I0816958

SOLO YO

First published in 2026 by OH
An Imprint of HEADLINE PUBLISHING GROUP LIMITED

1

Disclaimer:
All trademarks, copyright, quotations, company names, registered names, products, characters, logos and catchphrases used or cited in this book are the property of their respective owners. This book has not been licensed, approved, sponsored, or endorsed by Bad Bunny.

Cataloguing in Publication Data is available from the British Library

ISBN 978-1-03544-265-2

Compiled and written by: Malcolm Croft
Editorial: Phoebe Hills
Designed and typeset in Avenir by: Stephen Cary
Project manager: Russell Porter
Production: Clare Hennessy
Printed and bound in Canada

Headline's policy is to use papers that are natural, renewable and recyclable products and made from wood grown in well-managed forests and other controlled sources. The logging and manufacturing processes are expected to conform to the environmental regulations of the country of origin.

HEADLINE PUBLISHING GROUP LIMITED
An Hachette UK Company
Carmelite House, 50 Victoria Embankment, London EC4Y 0DZ

The authorised representative in the EEA is Hachette Ireland, 8 Castlecourt Centre, Dublin 15, D15 XTP3, Ireland (email: info@hbgi.ie)

www.headline.co.uk www.hachette.co.uk

SOLO YO

THE LITTLE GUIDE TO
BAD BUNNY

UNOFFICIAL AND UNAUTHORIZED

CONTENTS

INTRODUCTION

Rapper. Actor. Wrestler. Fashion icon. All-round good guy. It's official: the biggest Latin rap artist in the world is… Bad Bunny! Since surfing stylishly out across the Atlantic from Puerto Rico in 2016, Benito Antonio Martínez Ocasio—as his mother calls him—has redefined Latin music on a global scale, credited with pushing Spanish-language rap into the mainstream. His 2022 smash *Un Verano Sin Ti* ruled the US Billboard charts for 13 weeks—the first all-Spanish album ever to be so, well, BIG. The most-streamed artist on Spotify for four years straight, with an unbelievable *110 billion streams—READ THAT AGAIN!*—and three Grammy trophies (so far), BB's winning streak of staggering statistics speaks for itself. And he's only just turned 30.

Unapologetically authentic, genre-bending and proudly Puerto Rican, Bad Bunny has become more than just a musical superstar—he's the single most important cultural icon in the world right now, for everyone from straight machismos to the Latin queer community. He's got it all—and all eyes are on him. Thankfully, he's got the looks and style to match: he's the only man ever to appear solo on the cover of *Playboy*, after all.

This tiny tome is a big and bold celebration of Bad Bunny's ten-year tenure at the top of the pops, filled with his greatest hits of wisdom and wit, from his breakthrough beginnings in 2016 right up to his world-shaking, record-making Super Bowl Halftime Show in 2026—the most-watched event on the planet. So yeah, the future doesn't just belong to Bad Bunny—he *is* the future. And what he does next is anyone's guess.

It's Bad Bunny, baby! Enjoy!

CHAPTER ONE

VEGA BAJA BABY

Before the world knew his name, Benito Antonio Martínez Ocasio was just a kid from Vega Baja, Puerto Rico.

Between grocery store shifts and late-night SoundCloud uploads, he was quietly building an empire from his bedroom—beat by beat.

Let's bounce back to where it all began…

"I'm Benito Antonio Martínez Ocasio, I'm Puerto Rican, and I always make my dreams come true."

Bad Bunny, on his identity, interview with Jen Ortiz, *The Cut*, September 29, 2025

Bad Bunny, that name comes from a picture when I was six years old. And when I saw it, I thought I should name myself 'Bad Bunny'. It's a name I knew would market well.

Bad Bunny, parade.com, September 2024

When he was six, Bad Bunny dressed up as a bunny for an Easter event at school, but looked so grumpy in the photo his mom took of him that his friends jokingly called him a 'bad bunny'. The nickname stuck and when choosing his stage name years later, he felt Bad Bunny had the unexpected and contradictory quality that reflected his artistic style.

I always tell the story of when I was in school: if I was feeling lazy and I didn't want to get up, they'd threaten me with not being allowed to listen to Tego Calderón. Man, I'd get up so fast and get dressed. I'd be ready. 'You're not going to listen to Tego's song!' And I'd say, 'Okay, Mami, fine. I'm ready!'

”

Bad Bunny, on how powerfully he needs music in his life—particularly that of legendary Puerto Rican hip-hop MC and reggaetonero Tego Calderón, interview with Carina Chocano, *GQ*, May 24, 2022

My grandpa, the storyteller. He's the funniest. he's also named Benito. He's always making jokes. And also my whole family, from his side—they're always making jokes and making fun of each other... That's the environment that I grew up in. My mom is a very happy woman. Her brother, my uncle, was always making jokes and making us laugh. My auntie too. I think I have a lot of comedy from both sides of my family. But my grandpa is the boss. I [grew up in] a huge comedy school.

”

Bad Bunny, on his grandpa, the source of his distinct (and dark) sense of humor, interview with Suzy Exposito, i-D.com, September 10, 2025

I didn't care about breaking records or being No. 1. I wanted to make music for Puerto Rico.

Bad Bunny, on the motivation behind his earliest songwriting, interview with Leila Cobo, *Billboard*, October 1, 2025

I started to cry, and she thought it was because I was so excited. It was because I didn't want to go. I said, 'I don't want to leave. I'm never going to leave Puerto Rico.'

Bad Bunny, recalling a memory of when he was 12 and his mom surprised him with a trip to New York city—but he didn't want to leave, interview with Solcyré Burga & Andrew R. Chow, *Time*, January 5, 2025

Tego Calderón... Vico C... Daddy Yankee, Wisin & Yandel, Héctor El Father, René [Joglar]... Calle 13... Arcángel... Those were my guys.

Bad Bunny, on his earliest songwriting influences, interview with Benicio Del Toro, *Interview*, February 13, 2024

“

I’m a big salsa fan. When I was a child, my older cousins would put on reggaeton or other genres and I’d tell them, ‘No! I’m a *salsero*!’ and I’d throw down some moves. I wasn’t good at dancing to salsa, but I’d try. So as an adult, ironically, what I listen to the most on a daily basis is salsa.

”

Bad Bunny, on his love of salsa—and being a salsero!, interview with Benicio Del Toro, *Interview*, February 13, 2024

I always tell people that to understand the culture of Puerto Rico, you have to come here and experience it. Not many people know Puerto Rico is at a cultural peak right now, with lots of kids making art.

”

Bad Bunny, on Puerto Rico having a renaissance in world culture, interview with Patricia Tortolani, *Allure*, November 5, 2021

> I'd like to see Puerto Rico be more aware of what we're capable of. Most of the island's new generation is more conscientious. My dream is to see Puerto Rico develop within our own community, not with foreigners... but that us natives work together to shape the island's future.

Bad Bunny, on his dreams for Puerto Rico—as it gains global interest (in part thanks to him!), interview with Benicio Del Toro, *Interview*, February 13, 2024

I never saw my mom late for work. I saw her always on time. And I learned that. If there was a man who needed something fixed, my dad would go and fix it. My dad was the kind of guy who, if I had three pairs of tennis shoes and there was a little boy in the neighborhood who was missing them, he would give them to him. At that time I didn't understand and now when I grew up, wow.

Bad Bunny, on growing up in a hard-working and kind household, interview with Benjamín Torres Gotay, *El Nuevo Día*, September 22, 2025

I was never on a mission to become a star. It happened organically. I've never made a song saying, 'This is going to go worldwide.' I never made a song thinking, man, this is for the world. This is to capture the gringo audience. Never. On the contrary, I make songs as if only Puerto Ricans were going to listen to them. I still think I'm there making music, and it's for Puerto Ricans. I forget the entire world listens to me.

Bad Bunny, on making music for his community, interview with Carina Chocano, *GQ*, May 24, 2022

Love manifests itself in different ways. There's the love for your mom, which is infinite, of your family, friends... There's the love for what you do; that's why I'm here. If it doesn't move you, it's not love.

Bad Bunny, on love's multitude forms, interview with Ecleen Luzmila Caraballo, *Complex*, June 6, 2024

I dreamed about having this career. I'd come home from school and go straight to the computer, making beats and learning to record my own music. I'd sometimes say, 'Damn, if this isn't meant to be, I don't know what I'll do because I don't have another dream.'

99

Bad Bunny, on his dreams of being professional musician, interview with Benicio Del Toro, *Interview*, February 13, 2024

My father listened to tropical music. My mom liked merengue. My grandfather listened to old man's music, like bolero, bohemia. With my friends, I would listen to a lot of reggaeton and rock. I grew up around a lot of musical influences. I have a lot of rhythms in my head.

Bad Bunny, on a variety of childhood influences inspiring his signature sound, interview with Abby Aguirre, *W*, May 4, 2021

People see me as this giant superstar who has done all these things and is recognized. But nothing would be possible if my parents hadn't met, fell in love and had me.

Bad Bunny, on love and family, interview with Solcyré Burga and Andrew Chow, *Time*, January 5, 2025

My top five: Héctor Lavoe, Frankie Ruiz, Cheo Feliciano, Ismael Rivera, Celia Cruz, Tito Rojas and Tito Rodríguez.

Bad Bunny, on his top five salsa icons—a favorite genre of his, interview with Leila Cobo, *Billboard*, October 1, 2025

The way your grandma tells a story. That's art. The way friends craft inside jokes while shooting the shit courtside. That's art. The ingenuity your dad had to muster in order to fix your basketball net. That's art. Art of the everyday… We experience art every day but don't recognize it.

Bad Bunny, on life as art, interview with *Highsnobiety*, December 7, 2021

My look wasn't part of any specific plan. When I was starting to make my music, my style came as part of the process of liberating my mind and liberating spirit. Since I was young, I had it in me—I just had to liberate it.

Bad Bunny, on his iconic sense of style, interview with Patricia Tortolani, *Allure*, November 5, 2021

I can now say with certainty, thank God, that I don't think there's any kind of whirlwind that could change me or make me get a big head and believe my own hype.

Bad Bunny, on keeping both feet on the ground, interview with Benjamín Torres Gotay, *El Nuevo Día*, September 22, 2025

November 10, 2016

The day Bad Bunny uploaded his first song "Diles" to SoundCloud. Shortly after, he was discovered by Noah Assad, founder of Puerto Rico's Rimas Entertainment, and signed to the label.

At the time, Bad Bunny was working as a bagger in a grocery store in Vega Baja.

It was 500,000, then it was a million. It's exciting to throw out a song and hit refresh and see how many people have played it.

"

Bad Bunny, on uploading his first song "Diles" to SoundCloud in 2016—and his life changing overnight, interview with Carina Chocano, *GQ*, May 24, 2022

I feel like I'm an athlete representing Puerto Rico in the Olympics. It's… *diablo*.

Bad Bunny, on his role as global cultural ambassador for Puerto Rico, interview with Carina del Valle Schorske, *New York Times*, October 11, 2020

When a person is a dreamer, they never stop dreaming. With the time I'm on this Earth, I'm going to do something.

”

Bad Bunny, on his life's mission, interview with Mitchell Peters and Paula Mejía, Dazed Digital, September 5, 2024

In one week I got one million plays. Producers started calling me at work. I would go to the bathroom to respond to them!

”

Bad Bunny, on "Diles", his first upload to SoundCloud in 2016, starting to get attention online, interview with Suzy Exposito, *Rolling Stone*, May 14, 2020

I always made rhythms, tracks, beats. I was clear that I wanted to be an artist, but I wanted it to be serious. That's why I didn't upload songs until I felt as prepared as possible, at the flow level, at the rhythm level, at the lyric level.

Bad Bunny, on releasing his music only when he felt it was the right time, interview with Carina Chocano, *GQ*, May 24, 2022

I wasn't the kid who got involved in the streets. I liked to be at home with my family.

”

Bad Bunny, on being a good boy growing up in Vega Baja, Puerto Rico, interview with Suzy Exposito, *Rolling Stone*, May 14, 2020

I don't speak English well, but after a few drinks you can speak any language.

”

Bad Bunny, on English as his second language, interview with Leila Cobo, *Billboard*, March 23, 2018

CHAPTER TWO

A WHOLE NEW WORLD

With Bad Bunny making waves that stretched far beyond the Atlantic, he brought with him a new kind of sound—a genreless, borderless, and bilingual fusion of traditional

Latin rhythms and his own fearless charm, blurring together reggaeton, trap, pop, and poetry into something the world had never heard before.

Thanks to him, Latin rap was no longer underground...

“

When I had my very first hit, I really thought that was it. All that success that came afterward was crazy to me.

”

Bad Bunny, on success, interview with Leila Cobo, *Billboard*, October 1, 2025

> Some things change because it's impossible for them not to when you get a lot of success and a bunch of money you didn't have before. But my inner self, my person is intact.

Bad Bunny, on how fame and fortune has (not) changed him yet, interview with Carina Chocano, *GQ*, May 24, 2022

I received this drastic change when I was 22 years old. I started to see the world, to travel, to see money, to see luxury. And there was a moment when I was not present, disconnected. I wasn't happy with all the success I was having—I wasn't enjoying it.

A lot of people I loved weren't around me, I wasn't sharing with my family what I should have been sharing. In terms of my musical and artistic vision, I was not where I wanted to be. There were many things that happened and that I was able to overcome.

Bad Bunny, on the changes that came with his first flush with fame in 2016, interview with Benjamín Torres Gotay, *El Nuevo Día*, September 22, 2025

The songwriting process I like the most is the one where I feel it: it comes out naturally in the moment, without even knowing where the lyrics are coming from. But they come.

”

Bad Bunny, on the gift of receiving a song without knowing where it's from, interview with Abby Aguirre, *W*, May 4, 2021

People are like, 'Oh, Bad Bunny is breaking ground with gringos!' No. José Feliciano was breaking ground with gringos in the Seventies. He was doing worldwide tours, he was in London, singing in English, singing to Anglophone audiences.

Bad Bunny, on not being the first Latin star to have success in the mainstream, interview with Julyssa Lopez, *Rolling Stone*, June 21, 2023

Just before I released my first album, *X100PRE*—that's when I realized that my life had changed forever. That's when I confirmed it, accepted it, and when I knew that everything I was experiencing was what I was supposed to be.

”

Bad Bunny, on when he first knew he was going to become a global star, interview with Julyssa Lopez, *Rolling Stone*, December 23, 2020

Many times, when I want to express myself in a more political way, I do it in songs because it's the best way I can. That way every Puerto Rican can listen to it and come to their own conclusion and do their research and understand it the way they think best.

Bad Bunny, on being political through his music, interview with Solcyré Burga & Andrew R. Chow, *Time*, January 5, 2025

“

No one tells me what to do with my music. Real. My mom doesn’t tell what to say, how is someone else going to? The only person I cared about [in that regard] is my mom and she accepts me.

Bad Bunny, on his lyrics and the things he chooses to rap about, interview with Leila Cobo, *Billboard*, March 23, 2018

I have always been confident in myself, even before I became famous. I believed in myself, I didn't change who I was to get people to love me, and for that reason, my fans connected with me.

”

Bad Bunny, on his self-confidence reading as authenticity among his fans, interview with Thatiana Diaz, *Refinery29*, February 3, 2020

You're never going to know what I'm going to do. You will not know my next move.

”

Bad Bunny, on being delightfully unpredictable, interview with Andrew R. Chow & Mariah Espada, *Time*, March 28, 2023

For me, Spanish is fucking cool, more than English.

Bad Bunny, on singing and rapping in Spanish as his first language, interview with Lucas Villa, *Spin*, August 2, 2021

“

A lot of legends have performed at Coachella—but no one like me. There’s never been a Benito performing at Coachella. And that’s the cool thing for me.

”

Bad Bunny, on his debut headline performance at Coachella Festival—the festival’s first Spanish-language headliner, interview with Andrew R. Chow & Mariah Espada, *Time*, March 28, 2023

My family don't treat me any differently. They treat me the same. I see my aunts and they treat me just like always. 'Benito Antonio, God bless you, here, take this with you.'

Bad Bunny, on his family being unfussed by his overwhelming success and fame, interview with Benjamín Torres Gotay, *El Nuevo Día*, September 22, 2025

When I was little, I didn't sing in public. I sang twice in school, but I was dying of fear. And I never did a lot of performances, just maybe a few things at church. I was never in a play at school or anything like that. But I did like it. When I was alone in my room, I'd act by myself. Everything that I would play, I'd always imagine I was acting.

Bad Bunny, on his fear of performing as a child, interview with Julyssa Lopez, *Rolling Stone*, January 13, 2025

My hustle comes from the desire to continue to grow, to grow in music, to grow as an artist, to keep feeding the hunger of my fans with new music. That's what always keeps me pushing.

Bad Bunny, on musical growth, interview with Raquel Reichard, *The FADER*, March 21, 2018

I always believed in myself. I would tell myself, 'if I get this, I won't want anything else'. It was the only thing that interested me and the only thing I thought about. Now I didn't think I would get here so fast. I didn't think I would do so many great things in such a short time, but I always believed in myself. For real. And I think that's what helped me, that I never lost confidence in myself, my talent or what I was capable of.

Bad Bunny, on always believing in himself, interview with Raquel Reichard, *The FADER*, March 21, 2018

If I wasn't going anywhere with my music, I was going to work in the culinary arts. I saw cooking as something creative because sure, there are recipes, but there's also the opportunity to craft your own dishes, to create your own flavor.

Bad Bunny, on his career if his music never took off, interview with Benicio Del Toro, Interview, February 13, 2024

"

My style has always been my own, just like my flow.

"

Bad Bunny, on being unique in his style and music, interview with Raquel Reichard, *The FADER*, March 21, 2018

Bad Bunny Discography

1. ***X 100PRE*** (2018)
2. ***Oasis*** (with J Balvin, 2019)
3. ***YHLQMDLG*** (2020)
4. ***Las Que No Iban a Salir*** (2020)
5. ***El Último Tour del Mundo*** (2020)
6. ***Un Verano Sin Ti*** (2022)
7. ***Nadie Sabe Lo Que Va a Pasar Mañana*** (2023)
8. ***DeBÍ TiRAR MáS FOToS*** (2025)

Which is your favorite?

“

I didn’t go back to the old times; I brought the old times here.

”

Bad Bunny, on making traditional Latin musical styles (such as salsa, plena) fashionable again through his albums, interview with Suzy Exposito, *Rolling Stone*, May 14, 2020

I can connect with people. Part of why I've won over fans is because I'm honest, whether it's through songs about fucking around, or sex, or love, or about my sadness, or Puerto Rico. I don't want to be someone I'm not, and I reflect that in how I present myself on the streets and on social media, and in my interviews. I'm not being fake. I think people, no matter what language they speak, can feel it.

Bad Bunny, on his ability to connect with his fans through his music—and being authentic, interview with Benicio Del Toro, *Interview*, February 13, 2024

I can simply tell you that since I was a kid, I didn't like to look like anyone else.

Bad Bunny, on always wanting to look different, interview with Jasmine Garsd, NPR, January 3, 2019

I always say, to dress is like an art, like the music. You are the artist. You dress in the manner that you want and you demonstrate who you are or what you're like in your way of dressing. I tell everyone to just dress how they want.

”

Bad Bunny, on his iconic fashion sense, interview with Raquel Reichard, *The FADER*, March 21, 2018

When I'm on the mic, whether it's to record a song or when I'm improvising, ['Ey, Ey']... is my way of getting the rhythm of the track, like all the rappers who use the 'Yeah, yeah'. Sometimes I try to avoid it because I don't want to overuse it, but it always sneaks in.

Bad Bunny, on his famous catchphrase "Ey, Ey" in his songs, interview with Benicio Del Toro, *Interview*, February 13, 2024

"The long titles of my albums always have meaning. *No Me Quiero Ir De Aquí (I Don't Want to Leave Here)* resonates with anyone who had to leave their country or even those who never want to leave."

Bad Bunny, on the significance of his album titles—particularly *No Me Quiero Ir De Aquí (I Don't Want to Leave Here)*, interview with Leila Cobo, *Billboard*, October 1, 2025

I was super prepared for that first impact and for people to be confused. But just as I was prepared, I had a lot of faith that, in the end, people would understand me.

”

Bad Bunny, on being prepared for sudden success, interview with Isabelia Herrera, *GQ*, March 20, 2019

“The more pissed I am, the more I’m going to yell.”

Bad Bunny, on standing up for the issues he believes in, interview with Julyssa Lopez, *Rolling Stone*, January 13, 2025

CHAPTER THREE

READY TO RUMBLE

From "Soy Peor", his first big hit, to early collaborations with J Balvin and Ozuna, Bad Bunny's rise to fame was as fast and furious (and fearless) as any WWE wrestler he admires.

Let's get ready to rumble!

I've never sat to watch a recording of one of my concerts. Never. But my wrestling fight—I've watched it a hundred times. For like a week, I would go to bed watching it.

Bad Bunny, on his first WWE fight in the ring with Damien Priest for WWE Backlash in 2023, interview with Patricia Tortolani, *Allure*, November 5, 2021

My life has changed a lot. But at the same time, nothing has changed. I'm still the same person. I've grown a lot. I've learned and made mistakes, but I still have the same passion for what I do. I keep doing what I like.

”

Bad Bunny, on staying the same despite his meteoric levels of fame, interview with Lucas Villa, *Spin*, August 2, 2021

Most of the people who work with me in my day-to-day life, my personal crew, they're friends from high school and from childhood. My blood brothers. I'm traveling around the world, doing things that I could never have imagined, and can share it with people who believed in me since the beginning, long before turning into who I am today. No matter where in the world I am, they can make me feel at home.

”

Bad Bunny, on giving jobs to his childhood friends so he is always surrounded by people he trusts, interview with Benicio Del Toro, *Interview*, February 13, 2024

I want to put my life at risk in the ring. I felt like I didn't risk it enough in the ring, and I want to do it. I want to scare my mother.

99

Bad Bunny, on his infamous wrestling match against pro-Wrestler Damian Priest in May 2023 at the WWE Backlash event in San Juan, Puerto Rico, interview with Julyssa Lopez, *Rolling Stone*, January 13, 2025

You won't get to know the real me through a video on Instagram, an interview, or a TikTok. If you really want to get to know me, I invite you to my home.

”

Bad Bunny, on social media, interview with Julyssa Lopez, *Rolling Stone*, June 21, 2023

The way I work is kind of messy, but it works for me. I start with one idea, and as I go, other things pop up, and somehow everything fits together.

Bad Bunny, on his unique songwriting process, Interview with Leila Cobo, *Billboard*, October 1, 2025

“I don’t think twice when it comes to expressing myself. But that’s what makes me human. I’m going to talk, and whoever doesn’t like it doesn’t have to listen to me. I’ve never been scared to express myself, because that’s who I am, cabrón.”

Bad Bunny, on expressing himself loud and clear, interview with Julyssa Lopez, *Rolling Stone*, January 13, 2025

My mami and papi love my music. They're always listening to the radio waiting for one of my songs to come on. And when it does, they turn up the volume—and turn it back down when it's over.

99

Bad Bunny, on his biggest fans—his parents, interview with Julianne Escobedo Shepherd, *The FADER*, August 28, 2018

Sometimes I forget there are people that think I represent a town, a hood, a country—people expect the best from you. That's why, every time, I try to be just me. I'm being me, and if what I am is what you like, good. If not, there will be someone else who will come and do that for y'all.

Bad Bunny, on always remaining true to himself, interview with Julianne Escobedo Shepherd, *The FADER*, August 28, 2018

Bad Bunny's beloved hometown—and the inspiration for many of his songs—Vega Baja, is a beautiful coastal town on Puerto Rico's north shore.

It is famed for its stunning beaches, including its most famous spot: Playa Puerto Nuevo, a beach with a distinctive rock formation that creates a natural swimming pool, in the ocean.

The town also features the historic Casa Alonso Museum, filled with local art, and a charming plaza and city hall from the 1920s.

Fancy a trip?

“

When I started freestyling, everyone liked it and it was very funny, but in private I did it for real. Then people started to motivate me saying, 'Why don't you put out music, put it online, put it here, put it on Facebook, whatever whatever' and I went, 'No no no.' But little by little, something was working in my mind and I said, 'It's true, I need to put something out.'

”

Bad Bunny, on what prompted him to upload his music to SoundCloud in 2016, interview with Julianne Escobedo Shepherd, *The FADER*, August 28, 2018

There's this balance between capturing the moment and just living it. The other day, I was interacting with a fan and I went to blow her a kiss, but she missed it because she was trying to grab her phone. She lost the moment! I hope someone else saw it and told her.

Bad Bunny, on the importance of living in the moment, interview with Leila Cobo, *Billboard*, October 1, 2025

It's an incredible time to make music. I'm very involved in the creation of everything I do, in my music and in the direction of its videos.

Bad Bunny, on his desire for creative control across all areas of his career, interview with Raquel Reichard, *The FADER*, March 21, 2018

Wrestling has influenced me a lot, and I've applied that to my career. The style, the importance of having a trademark move or phrase or look, and always remembering the element of surprise. In wrestling, the fans love getting caught off guard. I like to create that same emotion with my music.

”

Bad Bunny, on the importance of wrestling on his musical career and fashion, interview with Patricia Tortolani, *Allure*, November 5, 2021

“I do everything, you know?”

Bad Bunny, on his multi-hyphenate talent—actor, comedian, style icon, producer, musician, interview with Raquel Reichard, *The FADER*, March 21, 2018

Music is a universal language. You have people from all parts of the world singing songs in Spanish. We don't have to sing in English anymore to cross over.

Bad Bunny, on fans crossing over to him—not the other way around, interview with Abby Aguirre, *W*, May 4, 2021

Bad Bunny has won three Grammy Awards. In 2021, he won Best Música Urbana Album for *YHLQMDLG* (*Yo Hago Lo Que Me Da La Gana*, or *I Do Whatever I Want*) marking a breakthrough for Spanish-language rap on the Grammy stage.

He followed with trophies in 2022 and 2023, including Best Música Urbana Album again for *Un Verano Sin Ti* (*A Summer Without You*).

These wins underscored not just his chart dominance but also the Grammy's recognition of reggaetón and Latin trap as powerful forces in global pop culture.

It was one of the more beautiful moments in my career, the recognition of an album that, for me, is very special, and which I consider one of the best albums in the latest era of reggaeton and the Latin genre.

Bad Bunny, on his first Grammy at the 2021 awards for Best Latin Pop or Urban Album for *Yo Hago Lo Que Me Da La Gana, or YHLQMDLG*, interview with Abby Aguirre, *W*, May 4, 2021

The fucking coronavirus arrived, and it sealed me up. People think I'm spending quarantine in a huge mansion with a really awesome pool… but I'm in an Airbnb.

Bad Bunny, on how he spent lockdown during the Covid-19 pandemic, interview with Suzy Exposito, *Rolling Stone*, May 14, 2020

In two years I've turned into a star, and that tells me that I can do a lot. If in two years I made myself a star, well, I expect that in two more I'll be able to make a mark. My only goal here is that the people will always remember my music and that they enjoy my music 20 years from now. I'm ready to make songs that don't die.

Bad Bunny, on his legacy, interview with Julianne Escobedo Shepherd, *The FADER*, August 28, 2018

I've never felt jealous in my life. In fact, the only time I've ever felt jealousy was when I saw the photo of Post Malone with [pro-wrestler] The Undertaker. Brooo, I almost cried! You saw he did the choke-slam on him?

”

Bad Bunny, on his passion for WWE wrestling, interview with Julianne Escobedo Shepherd, *The FADER*, August 28, 2018

It was such a special experience to represent the Latino community in an American event of the NFL. I don't know anything about the NFL. I don't know who won. Latinos won the game.

Bad Bunny, on being asked to perform at the 2020 Superbowl Half-time show with Shakira and Jennifer Lopez's co-headlining performance, interview with Griselda Flores, *Billboard*, February 29, 2020

I have many types of fans: fans from the LGBTQ community, and I'm sure also homophobic fans; feminists and machistas. I have the capacity to get them all hooked with reggaeton and this vocabulary. I talk the way we talk, and I give them a message without making them feel like it's a sermon.

Bad Bunny, on being an icon and a beacon of hope for the Latin queer community, interview with Lena Hansen, *People*, January 6, 2021

When I arrived, at first a lot of people were like, 'This kid is different'... I'd go to the studio with short shorts and flip-flops, and they'd say, '*Cabrón*, what's wrong with you?!'

Bad Bunny, on his distinct flair for style and fashion, interview with Isabelia Herrera, *GQ*, March 20, 2019

I don't care about fame. I don't care about that pressure that we were talking about. I don't care about that. I'm a person. I'm a human and I make mistakes. I have always said I will live how I want. But I never limit or act a way because of what they're going to say or think—no. I'm famous and I don't stop being human.

"

Bad Bunny, on his dissatisfaction with fame, interview with Andrew R. Chow & Mariah Espada, *Time*, March 28, 2023

Since childhood, I've been a clown. I've always liked being very funny or trying to make people laugh. It's my original self.

Bad Bunny, on always being an entertainer, interview with Julianne Escobedo Shepherd, *The FADER*, August 28, 2018

Puerto Rico is beautiful, but what makes it special is its culture. When people travel to the island, they're looking for gorgeous places and beaches, but you can find that anywhere. What gives the island its enchantment is our culture.

Bad Bunny, on what makes Puerto Rico so special, interview with Benicio Del Toro, *Interview*, February 13, 2024

It makes me really proud to get to this level by speaking in Spanish, and not only in Spanish, in the Spanish we speak in Puerto Rico, without changing my accent.

”

Bad Bunny, on not changing who he is and where he's from in order to be famous, interview with Lena Hansen, *People*, January 6, 2021

CHAPTER FOUR

KING CABRÓN

If there's one word to sum up Bad Bunny, it's cabrón — his favorite word, judging by his interviews...

Among friends, it means "badass" — its literal translation from Spanish being "male goat".

And what a GOAT he is... the greatest of all time...

There's so many things to say. I know they're probably going to cut me off, screw them. But to all the musicians, to all the people who belong to the Academy: With all my respects, reggaeton is part of Latin culture, and it's representing, just like lots of other music genres, Latinos around the world...

Also, I tell my colleagues from reggaeton, let's make an effort; let's bring back creativity and sincerity. The genre has become about views, numbers. Let's turn things around and do genuine things and different things for the people.

”

Bad Bunny, his first Grammy win acceptance speech in March 2021, receiving Best Latin Pop or Urban Album for *YHLQMDLG* (released in 2020)

“

I know what it is to be a normal kid, I know what life is like for young people.

”

Bad Bunny, on his upbringing and values, interview with Julianne Escobedo Shepherd, *The FADER*, August 28, 2018

Going shopping with my mom was one of my favorite things because I would get lost in the women's department. The women had it all! For women there are so many different types, colors, shapes, designs... And what do men get? The same jeans and T-shirts, jeans and T-shirts in different sizes and beat-up old wallet to stuff in your pocket.

Bad Bunny, on preferring clothes shopping in the women's section, interview with Patricia Tortolani, *Allure*, November 5, 2021

If I'm playing chess, I want to win. If I'm making jokes, I want to tell better jokes. I'm very competitive. In all situations. So obviously in music I am. But in a good way. If I see someone making a badass song, I am going to make a more badass song. I want to do something better. But not to overshadow them, but because I want to do something better. We can all win, we can all shine together.

”

Bad Bunny, on his competitive streak being a positive thing, interview with Andrew R. Chow & Mariah Espada, *Time*, March 28, 2023

> “From 2016 to 2018 I disappeared. I was inside a capsule; I didn’t find out about anything. The world would see me but I had disappeared.”

Bad Bunny, on not enjoying his first taste of fame—and exiling himself for two years, interview with Lena Hansen, *People*, January 6, 2021

When people expect something from me, I like to go in the other direction.

Bad Bunny, on being unpredictable, interview with Kate Linthicum, *LA Times*, February 28, 2020

“

I remember two years ago I told myself, papi, I’m already at a level that I won’t be able to recover my normal life.

”

Bad Bunny, on being too famous to ever have a normal life again, interview with Andrew R. Chow & Mariah Espada, *Time*, March 28, 2023

I create an entire world: from the videos, the visuals, the cover, the thematics, everything synchronized, with the purpose that you listen to it so that you feel like you're in a particular place. If someone is in fucking Switzerland, my music will make them feel like they're in the Caribbean. If you are in Puerto Rico even better—you are already there.

Bad Bunny, on his music embodying the spirit of Puerto Rico, interview with Andrew R. Chow & Mariah Espada, *Time*, March 28, 2023

“

I always look luxurious.

”

Bad Bunny, on his iconic and distinct fashion sense, interview with Suzy Exposito, *Rolling Stone*, May 14, 2020

What's the point in being here? What's the point of being at this level? What do I win? I'll die and that's it—I'm not going to take anything with me. So I think that's it: to show the world who I am and what my culture is, where I grew up.

”

Bad Bunny, on his mission with his life and music, interview with Julyssa Lopez, *Rolling Stone*, January 13, 2025

In 2022, Bad Bunny made streaming history when he was named Spotify's most-streamed artist three years in a row.

Today, he has amassed almost 110 billion streams on Spotify alone, with more than 115 million equivalent album sales!

I had a show in Rome, in the south of Italy, where the language is obviously not Spanish. But the people who didn't know Spanish were singing my songs. It was something incredible, something that made me go, 'Wow, we're doing things well, making good music for another culture, another language to get involved in the movement.'

Bad Bunny, on when he first realized his music had crossed language barriers (without him having to compromise), interview with Caitlin Donohue, *Remezcla*, July 25, 2017

I met some millionaires and when I told them where I was from, Puerto Rico, they said, 'oh, great, taxes'. I felt like, it's so fucked up, that I say Puerto Rico and the first thing this gringo says is, 'oh, yeah, taxes'.

Bad Bunny, on Puerto Rico being a tax haven, exempt from US federal income tax, interview with Benjamín Torres Gotay, *El Nuevo Día*, September 22, 2025

"Latino culture is very *machista*. So, that's why I think everything that I've done has been even more shocking. People think that if you're a reggaeton artist, you have to act or dress a certain way. But why? If I dress this way, I can't sing this way? Or if I dress like this, I can't listen to this type of music?"

Bad Bunny, on breaking the mold and smashing stereotypes of Latin culture, interview with Carina Chocano, *GQ*, May 24, 2022

Bad Bunny has put Latin music on the map in a way no other Latin artist had done before him.

His vibrant fusion of beats includes salsa, plena, bomba, reggaeton, bachata, merengue, cumbia, tango, samba, bossa nova, and Latin pop, musical forms rooted in African, Indigenous, and Spanish traditions, and ranging from the sensual (bachata) to explosive (salsa) to the rapid dembow rhythms of reggaeton.

I love percussion—drums, conga, bongos. There's something in me that's always loved that. I think there's something in my DNA that's calling me.

”

Bad Bunny, on his passions for different rhythms, interview with Julyssa Lopez, *Rolling Stone*, January 13, 2025

I always dreamed about people listening and recognizing my music, and to be able to make a living from it. But even though I dreamed about it deep in my heart, I never expected to get to this level so far.

Bad Bunny, on the unexpected and overwhelming success he's achieved, interview with Julyssa Lopez, *Rolling Stone*, January 13, 2025

I have always felt like there was a part of me that is very feminine. But I never felt as masculine as I did the day I dressed up like a drag queen.

”

Bad Bunny, on his 2020 music video for the song "Yo Perreo Sola", which was celebrated as a statement against machismo and for LGBTQ+ rights, interview with Suzy Exposito, *Rolling Stone*, May 14, 2020

I grew up with a lot of love from my mother and my father. I saw them sometimes trying hard, going through difficult times to bring us food and other times, easy. They were beautiful moments, sometimes of uncertainty but in the end I was always grateful to the core that I grew up in my family, and the way I grew up because from there I acquired a lot of experience and a lot of knowledge that makes me the person I am today.

Bad Bunny, on his happy childhood, interview with Andrew R. Chow & Mariah Espada, *Time*, March 28, 2023

When I was a little boy, I only dreamed of music and that someone would listen to my music. I always say that if a thousand people listened to me and I performed once a month at a little place, just with that I would be happy. But the hunger and the passion that I have for this is impossible because I always want to give more and more and more.

Bad Bunny, on fame, success and wanting more, interview with Andrew R. Chow & Mariah Espada, *Time*, March 28, 2023

I always like to create things that get attention. It used to be a problem when I wasn't famous. Now, I can do whatever I want and people have to accept it.

Bad Bunny, on his signature sound, look and style, interview with Jasmine Garsd, NPR, January 3, 2019

My sound is not like a new rhythm, it's a very old rhythm, it just sounds new and different because I'm doing it—I'm making this sound with my voice, my style, my flow. Sometimes young people can think, and I used to think... this type of music is for old people, that's my abuelita's or my grandpa's music. But when you grow up, you start to appreciate it and understand it more...

I just want to let them know that you can make it in a very cool way... like your own style. You don't have to do the same thing that the old artists did in the past. You can do it with a new feeling, with a new slang, with a new everything. There's no rules.

Bad Bunny, on reinventing traditional Latin/Puerto Rican music or a new generation, interview with Jon Caramanica and Joe Coscarelli, *New York Times*, January 5, 2025

Someone will ask me for a photo, I stretch out my hand, and they leave it there because they're looking for their phone. I'm a human. Greet me. The photo isn't worth more than a greeting. A photo isn't worth more than an exchange of words. That's worth more than a photo. You can say I know Bad Bunny. You prefer to know me or have a picture with me?

Bad Bunny, on interacting with his fans, interview with Andrew R. Chow & Mariah Espada, *Time*, March 28, 2023

I make music like I'm the only person in the world.

Bad Bunny, on not thinking about success or fame when recording music in his studio, interview with Andrew R. Chow & Mariah Espada, *Time*, March 28, 2023

“

Now that I’ve reached *this* level, I’ve earned the freedom to chase even my wildest ideas.

”

Bad Bunny, on his wild aspirations for his career, interview with Thania Garcia, *Variety*, June 18, 2025

I've been listening to a lot of Chuito el de Bayamón, an artist from Puerto Rico from the '40s and '50s and all the songs are about things I can relate to. 'Wait, he's singing about this—I was living that two weeks ago.'

Bad Bunny, on relating to music made before he was born, interview with Jon Caramanica and Joe Coscarelli, *New York Times*, January, 5, 2025

CHAPTER FIVE

WORLD'S HOTTEST

As Spotify's most-streamed artist from 2020 to 2022, Bad Bunny is truly the world's hottest musician — no one can touch him.

And yet, fame, fortune, and glory all pale in comparison to his one true purpose: being a proud Puerto Rican...

I could have done a track with, who knows, Miley Cyrus or Katy Perry. But no, I was making 'Safaera' with Ñengo Flow and Jowell y Randy. And I was putting the whole world onto underground from Puerto Rico, you know? That makes me feel proud of what I represent.

”

Bad Bunny, on preferring to shine a light on new underground Latino artists over collaborating with mainstream American artists, interview with Isabelia Herrera, *New York Times*, May 6, 2022

You never get used to that. It never becomes normal. It will always cause emotions to see people get so excited and receive you that way. It changes you.

Bad Bunny, on how he feels when people scream his name at live shows, interview with Carina Chocano, *GQ*, May 24, 2022

"No matter the era I had been born during, I would have been great."

Bad Bunny, on the timelessness of both his music and himself, interview with Julyssa Lopez, *Rolling Stone*, January 13, 2025

Every time that I express myself about something, I do it because I feel it. It's not because I'm Bad Bunny and I have 40 million followers. I'm a normal human being and I have feelings and I get mad and I get happy and that's how I make my music. Sometimes you want to cry, sometimes you want to dance, sometimes you want to fall in love and sometimes you want to talk about political things. That's how it works: Everything that I say and everything that I do is because I feel it, not because I feel a pressure to say something because I'm a public figure.

Bad Bunny, on being a normal human being with emotions, interview with Jon Caramanica and Joe Coscarelli, *New York Times*, January, 5, 2025

Today, everyone's a paparazzi. We're in the worst time, the worst moment for the privacy of other humans; not just artists, but human beings. Today, no one respects the privacy or life of anyone.

Bad Bunny, on social media and fan intrusion in his personal life, interview with Julyssa Lopez, *Rolling Stone*, June 21, 2023

At times, I do think, cabrón, what I'm signing up for is a lot. But the way I see it, I'm not a doctor; I'm not a teacher; I'm not someone who has to wake up every morning at 5 a.m. to lay down concrete on a busy road to survive. My job is to fucking sing, and even though it comes with its own set of sacrifices, it feels silly to complain about it.

Bad Bunny, on his job being low stakes compared to others, interview with Thania Garcia, *Variety*, June 18, 2025

I always say that I had a very normal life. I grew up with my mom and dad. I am the oldest brother of three. When my first brother Bernie came and the second, Bysael. My mother was a teacher and my dad was a truck driver. So you know we were working people. Very Catholic. We went to church.

Bad Bunny, on his normal upbringing, interview with Andrew R. Chow & Mariah Espada, *Time*, March 28, 2023

Bad Bunny Dictionary

1. ***Cabrón*** – badass (literally "male goat")
2. ***Mami*** – hottie
3. ***Chavos*** – money
4. ***Perreo*** – a reggaeton grinding dance style
5. ***Bicho*** – slang for penis
6. ***Corillo*** – group of friends, or crew/inner circle
7. ***Dura*** – a strong, amazing woman
8. ***Bellaquear*** – to flirt
9. ***Latigazo*** – whip or twerk dance move
10. ***Janguear*** – to hang out
11. ***Safaera*** – freaky fun
12. ***Bebesita*** – baby girl
13. ***Perrear*** – to twerk

We are in a digital era where there is a lot of content—every day, new music comes out from different parts of the world, from new talents, from veterans, from all over the world. Today, a year is equivalent to five or three months within social networks or in the music industry. But I do not see this as pressure. It has come naturally to me releasing so many albums. It's not like: 'I have to put out music now'—it happens naturally.

”

Bad Bunny, on having released five albums in just two years—unheard of!, interview with Julyssa Lopez, *Rolling Stone*, December 23, 2020

I would rather you just leave. Because here we all are having fun, we are talking, we are joking, we are telling stories, anecdotes, talking about our experiences, and you are on fucking Twitter or fucking Facebook.

”

Bad Bunny, on people constantly being on their phone—which he loathes, interview with Laia Garcia-Furtado, *Vulture*, November 22, 2021

On September 28, 2025, Apple Music, the NFL and Roc Nation announced that Bad Bunny would headline the Super Bowl LX halftime show on February 8, 2026, marking the spectacle's 60th anniversary.

This would be Bad Bunny's second time on the Super Bowl stage, after featuring as a guest during Shakira and Jennifer Lopez's 2020 halftime show.

I'm really excited for my friends, my family, Puerto Rico, all the Latino people around the world. I'm excited about my culture. I'm excited about everything, not just for me. I'm going to enjoy. I'm going to embrace the moment. I'm going to show what we have, our music, our culture. I'm just going to the stage to enjoy and have fun.

Bad Bunny, on the significance of his Super Bowl LX Halftime Show performance in 2026—and knowing all eyes will be on him for 15 minutes, interview with Zane Lowe, Apple Music, September 25, 2025

When I finish a song, I analyze what can be improved, what does not sound good enough, or what could sound better. The same happens with production, I'm always trying new things, new ideas, so it is something that I am passionate about. When you do things with that passion and love, it shows.

Bad Bunny, on the quality of the production and sound of his music—and constantly trying new things to elevate it, interview with Julyssa Lopez, *Rolling Stone*, December 23, 2020.

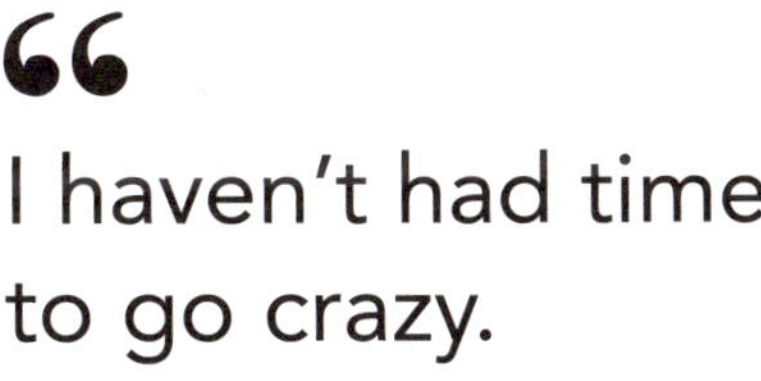

“I haven’t had time to go crazy.”

Bad Bunny, on his swift ascension to superstardom, interview with Lena Hansen, *People*, January 6, 2021

I need to come up with new hobbies. I don't have a hobby that isn't music—it's my work, my play, my way of relaxing. I need to sit down and find some other stuff to do.

”

Bad Bunny, on wanting to try acting, interview with Julyssa Lopez, *Rolling Stone*, December 23, 2020

The stage is where I'm the most present and happiest. I'll probably be doing this until I'm an old man.

Bad Bunny, on his love of performing, interview with Thania Garcia, *Variety*, June 18, 2025

I've made it clear to people that I'm never going to make a record that's the same as another.

Bad Bunny, on never repeating himself artistically, interview with Isabelia Herrera, *New York Times*, May 6, 2022

If I ever feel pressure, it's because it's coming from me. If I want to do something better, it's because of me. I don't let myself give into pressure from other people, I don't feel pressure to be the best. Never, ever, ever. I do this because I love it.

Bad Bunny, on internal pressure, interview with Julyssa Lopez, *Rolling Stone*, June 21, 2023

At the end of the day, I don't know if in 20 years I will like a man. One never knows. But at the moment I am heterosexual and I like women.

Bad Bunny, on his sexuality, interview with Ben Hoyle, *The Times*, January 2, 2021

I like to perform like nobody there knows who I am or what I've accomplished.

Bad Bunny, on his live performance philosophy, interview with Thania Garcia, *Variety*, June 18, 2025

I just wash my face with the same body wash I use to wash my ass. I don't do anything... I'm blessed.

Bad Bunny, on his skincare routine (or lack thereof!), interview with Alyssa Morin, E Online, October 27, 2020

Everybody has to feel comfortable with what they are. What defines a man, what defines being masculine, what defines being feminine? To me, a dress is a dress. If I wear a dress, would it stop being a woman's dress? Or vice versa? Like, no. It's a dress, and that's it. It's not a man's, it's not a woman's. It's a dress.

Bad Bunny, on his genderless approach to clothing, interview with Carina Chocano, *GQ*, May 24, 2022

I say to the people: I'm Hollywood, but I'm also Puerto Rico. I'm also the hood. I can talk to these Hollywood people, and the next day I will be in the hood with my flag, with my swag, with my Puerto Rican slang.

Bad Bunny, on living the best of both worlds, interview with Suzy Exposito, i-D.com, September 10, 2025

When they first showed me the routing for the stadium tour, I was like, 'Two nights in Sweden?!' Bro, I thought it was a prank.

”

Bad Bunny, on being a global phenomenon, interview with Thania Garcia, *Variety*, June 18, 2025

I remember for my first video, the directors were saying, 'Who the fuck is this guy and why is he dressing like this?' People went crazy because I was wearing short shorts.

”

Bad Bunny, on having a distinct fashion sense from the very start of his career, interview with Ben Hoyle, *The Times*, January 2, 2021

I don't remember the first song that I wrote, but I'm sure it had to do with stories that were a little sad and heartbreak.

Bad Bunny, on his first song he wrote, interview with Mitchell Peters, Paula Mejía, Dazed Digital, September 5, 2024

“

I don’t know if this is a good or bad habit yet, but I prefer not to think about the numbers or the weight of everything. Because then I start, ‘Should I be proud? Should I be nervous? Should I just act like this is totally normal for me?’

”

Bad Bunny, on trying not to think about how successful he is and how many streams he has or albums he's sold, interview with Thania Garcia, *Variety*, June 18, 2025

It's very special to be able to achieve my dreams simply by doing what I love.

Bad Bunny, on living his dreams, interview with Abby Aguirre, *W*, May 4, 2021

CHAPTER SIX

EL CONEJO MALO

Bad Bunny has redefined stardom for the 21st century: a bedroom musician from one of the world's smallest islands turned global music disruptor in just a few short years.

Today, he's not just a musician — he's a mirror for a new generation: strong yet vulnerable, male but not masculine, political yet playful.

His legacy isn't just in his hits; it's in the humanity he's reminded the world to feel.

This is for you, El Conejo Malo...

Bad Bunny represents a dream come true. It represents the freedom to do what I always wanted to do. To be the person I always wanted to be, or maybe the person I always was, but that the world didn't fully understand... I want my music to be a part of people's special moments. Whether they're sad or happy moments, I want my music to be their companions. And with that, I am satisfied.

”

Bad Bunny, on what Bad Bunny represents, interview with *Highsnobiety*, December 7, 2021

Bad Bunny's most streamed song, "DÁKITI", has more than 2.3 billion streams. Released in October 2020 with Jhay Cortez, its title refers to a chill beach vibe and Puerto Rican nightlife.

Two other Bad Bunny tracks have also surpassed two billion streams: "LA CANCIÓN" and "Me Porto Bonito". Over 20 other of his songs have more than a billion streams!

I read people extremely well. I'm very intuitive with who and how I spend my time. I take care of my mental and heart space.

Bad Bunny, on looking after his health and his heart, interview with Thania Garcia, *Variety*, June 18, 2025

Maybe my music isn't wholesome. But I didn't invent sex nor marijuana.

Bad Bunny, on the candid and sometimes controversial elements of his lyrics, interview with Paula Mejía, Dazed Digital, September 5, 2021

It didn't matter your musical taste, your political views or anything else. This was for everyone. I wanted people to look back and say, 'I was part of that'. The whole concept was about respecting and loving each other and also taking care of our home and our culture. Everyone was welcome. Across 30 shows, there wasn't a single viral video of people fighting or arguing. Everyone was just happy, dancing and showing love.

Bad Bunny, on the cultural significance of his 31-show residency at Coliseo de Puerto Rico José Miguel Agrelot in San Juan, Puerto Rico between July-September 2025, interview with Leila Cobo, *Billboard*, October 1, 2025

My mom didn't know I was making two movies [*Been Caught Stealing* & *Happy Gilmore*] and when I told her, she was so happy. She was like, 'You have no idea how glad it makes me to hear these things. When you were little, even though you loved music, I never imagined you'd be a musical artist. I always imagined you as an actor.'

Bad Bunny, on his mother's belief that he would grow up to be an actor, interview with Julyssa Lopez, *Rolling Stone*, January 13, 2025

My first kiss for a movie and it was with a man. That's the penalty I get for being with so many women during my life.

Bad Bunny, on his first acting experience with Gael García Bernal in the 2023 film *Cassandro*, where he played Felipe, a love interest of Bernal's character, Saúl Armendáriz, interview with Andrew R. Chow & Mariah Espada, *Time*, March 28, 2023

Bad Bunny is making waves as an actor too. He made his debut in *Narcos: Mexico* (2021) as stylish hitman Arturo "Kitty" Páez, before appearing alongside Brad Pitt in action movie *Bullet Train* (2022) as vengeful assassin "The Wolf".

He was also cast as Colorado in *Caught Stealing* (2025), directed by Darren Aronofsky, alongside Austin Butler and Zoë Kravitz and as hipster golfer Oscar in Adam Sandler's hit sequel *Happy Gilmore* (2025).

“Brad Pitt was super fire. Sometimes, during filming, they’d yell ‘Cut!’ and I would think, What the fuck. I’m here with Brad Pitt!”

Bad Bunny, on working with Brad Pitt for 2022’s *Bullet Train*, interview with Carina Chocano, *GQ*, May 24, 2022

"

I [did] acting stuff before, but I was a criminal (*Narcos*) or it was an action movie (*Bullet Train*) so this [*Happy Gilmore*] is my first opportunity in a comedy movie. That's the type of movie that I always watched since I was a kid. Especially Adam Sandler movies, [he's] my favorite actor of all time.

"

Bad Bunny, on acting in comedy movies and his love of Adam Sandler, interview with Suzy Exposito, i-D.com, September 10, 2025

I was [filming] *Been Caught Stealing*, I was doing *Happy Gilmore 2*, and I had never been so far from Puerto Rico for so long. It drove me to [research] my roots, to connect with everything I am as a Puerto Rican.

”

Bad Bunny, on leaving Puerto Rico to film back-to-back Hollywood movies, interview with Suzy Exposito, i-D.com, September 10, 2025

I don't want to rush into a big role when I still feel like I'm not at that level yet. I want to win those roles according to my skills and work my way through the industry step by step.

”

Bad Bunny, on taking his time with his acting career, interview with Benicio Del Toro, *Interview*, February 13, 2024

A lot of artists fail when they try to act, and they flop. So when I get into acting, it's going to be to do it well, something good, something of quality. I want people to say, 'Wow.'

Bad Bunny, on taking his time to nurture his acting career, interview with Isabelia Herrera, *GQ*, March 20, 2019

I always ask myself, 'How can I entertain and surprise people with something new?' And that's the pressure, but it's a positive internal pressure.

”

Bad Bunny, on constantly trying to surprise his fans—and himself, interview with *Highsnobiety*, December 7, 2021

“I just turned 30—I can say I’m old, I can say I’m young.”

Bad Bunny, on aging and the experience it brings, interview with Paula Mejía, Dazed Digital, September 5, 2024

That's what I love most about what I do: thinking about what's next. I'm not focused on reaching some higher level of greatness. I just want to create from the heart and let life, the world and the people decide what it becomes.

Bad Bunny, on letting his heart lead his art, interview with Leila Cobo, *Billboard*, October 1, 2025

"

I'm pleased that we are in a time where I don't need to change anything about myself—not my musical style, not my language, not my culture—to go far. That doesn't mean I'll never sing in English. I already sang in Japanese, so maybe one day I'll sing in English. It feels great to do things my way.

"

Bad Bunny, on not having to change who he is in order to be understood by fans worldwide, interview with Lucas Villa, *Spin*, August 2, 2021

I’ve never been a great dancer, but I always liked salsa. I know the basics, so if I get drunk I could dance the whole night. But I like to dance because I feel the music, you know? It’s like a body language, a soul language.

Bad Bunny, on his love of dancing, interview with Suzy Exposito, i-D.com, September 10, 2025

If I look back now I can say I've done everything, but if I look to the future I haven't done anything.

”

Bad Bunny, on feeling wise—depending on which way you look!, interview with Paula Mejía, Dazed Digital, September 5, 2024

I don't take the critics seriously—the good ones I carry with me. The bad ones, sometimes you read them and you think, *Damn, they're right*. You realize they aren't bad reviews, just valid criticism. Then there's people who are on a crazy trip, and you have to ignore them.

Bad Bunny, on reading the reviews of his albums and live shows, interview with Laia Garcia-Furtado, *Vulture*, November 22, 2021

I had the desire for a long time to try to make a salsa album. But I always thought about it for the future—like, 'maybe when I'm 40'. But why wait so long?

Bad Bunny, on his desire to make a proper salsa album—to pay tribute to his favorite genre, interview with Suzy Exposito, i-D.com, September 10, 2025

I do music for the people that love me and for who wants to connect with me. If you don't like what I'm doing—go somewhere else.

Bad Bunny, on not caring about trying to please people who don't like his music, interview with Andrew R. Chow & Mariah Espada, *Time*, March 28, 2023

My sound is the sound of now, and of the future. It's a party, it's nostalgia, it's struggle… it's romance.

Bad Bunny, when asked "What does your music sound like to you?", interview with Suzy Exposito, i-D.com, September 10, 2025

I could sing in whatever flow, but I want people to say, 'This is Bad Bunny.' your trap and reggaeton songs could easily be translated into ballads or pop songs.

99

Bad Bunny, on having a signature sound regardless of genre, interview with Julyssa Lopez, *Rolling Stone*, January 13, 2025

I've done a lot of shows here in Puerto Rico, and I don't think I've felt so much energy before. The pride, the sense of homeland that unites generations.

”

Bad Bunny, on his now-legendary 31-date show at Coliseo de Puerto Rico José Miguel Agrelot in San Juan, Puerto Rico between July-September 2025, interview with Suzy Exposito, i-D.com, September 10, 2025

Bad Bunny's *No Me Quiero Ir de Aquí* (*I Don't Want to Leave Here*) residency in San Juan's Coliseo de Puerto Rico is a record-breaking celebration of his roots.

Across 31 shows, Bad Bunny performed to more than 600,000 fans—two-thirds of whom were from overseas—and boosted the island's economy by more than $400 million!

Tickets sold out in just four hours.

“

I think it’s my responsibility, as a person of influence—not just as an artist but as a person—to sometimes try to do what I can. If I have the chance to say something, I will say it—but that doesn’t obligate me to always say something, or to shed light on every problem, as if I were a lawmaker.

”

Bad Bunny, on his responsibility as a role model, interview with Isabelia Herrera, GQ, March 20, 2019

[*Debí Tirar Más Fotos*] is an album of Puerto Rican music, and a completely different vibe from what any other artist has done. I found what my roots are: the sound that represents me.

Bad Bunny, on the significance of the sound and genre of his groundbreaking 2025 album *Debí Tirar Más Fotos*, interview with Solcyré Burga & Andrew R. Chow, *Time*, January 5, 2025

"

It's not until someone comes up to me and tells me, 'Man, thank you', that I realize the impact of what I do.

"

Bad Bunny, on the impact of his music with his fans, interview with Jessica Roiz, *Billboard*, July 7, 2020

I want people to remember me as someone genuine, someone with a big heart. For being myself. That's what leaving your mark is about, doing something that represents who you really are.

Bad Bunny, on how he'd like to be remembered, interview with Lucas Villa, *Spin*, August 2, 2021

At the beginning I did what I could. Now I do whatever I want.

”

Bad Bunny, on being successful enough to do as he pleases, interview with Isabelia Herrera, *GQ*, March 20, 2019

Every day, something new comes out: 'Bad Bunny did this. Bad Bunny achieved this. No. 1 here, No. 1 there. Bad Bunny broke a record!' And it feels good, it feels amazing, but it's like: 'Fuck, enough is enough, dude! Give me a break! It's just too much!'

Bad Bunny, on the overwhelming volume of complimentary media attention, fame and success, interview with Julyssa Lopez, *Rolling Stone*, December 23, 2020

I am Puerto Rican, I am Caribbean, and my music, my culture, my country's history run through my veins, from plena to reggaeton. At the peak of my career and popularity, I want to show the world who I am, who BENITO ANTONIO is, and who PUERTO RICO is.

Bad Bunny, on his pride for his homeland and heritage, *Billboard*, January 5, 2025